Great

I think the series is wonderful and beneficial for tourists to get information before visiting the city.

-Seckin Zumbul, Izmir Turkey

I am a world traveler who has read many trip guides but this one really made a difference for me. I would call it a heartfelt creation of a local guide expert instead of just a guide.

-Susy, Isla Holbox, Mexico

New to the area like me, this is a must have!

-Joe, Bloomington, USA

This is a good series that gets down to it when looking for things to do at your destination without having to read a novel for just a few ideas.

-Rachel, Monterey, USA

Good information to have to plan my trip to this destination.

-Pennie Farrell, Mexico

Great ideas for a port day.

-Mary Martin USA

Tracy Carmen Watkin

Aptly titled, you won't just be a tourist after reading this book. You'll be greater than a tourist!

-Alan Warner, Grand Rapids, USA

Thank you for a fantastic book.

-Don, Philadelphia, USA

Even though I only have three days to spend in San Miguel in an upcoming visit, I will use the author's suggestions to guide some of my time there. An easy read - with chapters named to guide me in directions I want to go.

-Robert Catapano, USA

Great insights from a local perspective! Useful information and a very good value!

-Sarah, USA

This series provides an in-depth experience through the eyes of a local. Reading these series will help you to travel the city in with confidence and it'll make your journey a unique one.

-Andrew Teoh, Ipoh, Malaysia

GREATER THAN A TOURIST – BARCELONA CATALUNYA SPAIN

50 Travel Tips from a Local

Tracy Carmen Watkin

Tracy Carmen Watkin

Cover designed by: Lisa Rusczyk Ed. D.
Cover Image:
https://pixabay.com/get/ea37b3092ef7083ecd1f4603e14d4e9efe76e7d71db9124891f3c3/barcelona-3226639.jpg

Greater Than a Tourist
Visit our website at www.GreaterThanaTourist.com

Lock Haven, PA

ISBN: 9781980733492

> TOURIST

50 TRAVEL TIPS FROM A LOCAL

Tracy Carmen Watkin

BOOK DESCRIPTION

Are you excited about planning your next trip?

Do you want to try something new?

Would you like some guidance from a local?

If you answered yes to any of these questions, then this Greater Than a Tourist book is for you.

Greater Than a Tourist – Barcelona, Catalunya, Spain by Tracy Carmen Watkin offers the inside scoop on Barcelona. Most travel books tell you how to travel like a tourist. Although there is nothing wrong with that, as part of the Greater Than a Tourist series, this book will give you travel tips from someone who has lived at your next travel destination.

In these pages, you will discover advice that will help you throughout your stay. This book will not tell you exact addresses or store hours but instead will give you excitement and knowledge from a local that you may not find in other smaller print travel books.

Travel like a local. Slow down, stay in one place, and get to know the people and the culture. By the time you finish this book, you will be eager and prepared to travel to your next destination.

Tracy Carmen Watkin

TABLE OF CONTENTS

Tracy Carmen Watkin

Tracy Carmen Watkin

DEDICATION

This book is dedicated to my husband, Jeff, who took this crazy adventure across an ocean with me.

Tracy Carmen Watkin

ABOUT THE AUTHOR

Tracy Carmen Watkin grew up in California and caught the travel bug from her parents at a young age. In 2008, she and her husband, Jeff, went on a trip to Paris and the Czech Republic with her family. This is where she began to look at Europe as more than just a place to visit. By 2011, they were living in Barcelona.

Tracy loves this city dearly, it has become 'home'. She loves helping people plan trips to Barcelona and connecting them with some of the secrets that only the locals know. Barcelona is a popular tourist destination, but without some local insight, you can miss many of the wonderful aspects of what makes this city so special.

When she's not writing, you can find Tracy hiking in the nearby mountains just outside of Barcelona, or working in her garden alongside her husband and pup.

Tracy Carmen Watkin

HOW TO USE THIS BOOK

The Greater Than a Tourist book series was written by someone who has lived in an area for over three months. The goal of this book is to help travelers either dream or experience different locations by providing opinions from a local. The author has made suggestions based on their own experiences. Please do your own research before traveling to the area in case the suggested places are unavailable.

Tracy Carmen Watkin

FROM THE PUBLISHER

Traveling can be one of the most important parts of a person's life. The anticipation and memories that you have are some of the best. As a publisher of the Greater Than a Tourist book series, as well as the popular 50 Things to Know book series, we strive to help you learn about new places, spark your imagination, and inspire you. Wherever you are and whatever you do I wish you safe, fun, and inspiring travel.

Lisa Rusczyk Ed. D.
CZYK Publishing

Tracy Carmen Watkin

OUR STORY

Traveling is a passion of the "Greater than a Tourist" series creator. Lisa studied abroad in college, and for their honeymoon Lisa and her husband toured Europe. During her travels to Malta, an older man tried to give her some advice based on his own experience living on the island since he was a young boy. She was not sure if she should talk to the stranger but was interested in his advice. When traveling to some places she was wary to talk to locals because she was afraid that they weren't being genuine. Through her travels, Lisa learned how much locals had to share with tourists. Lisa created the "Greater Than a Tourist" book series to help connect people with locals. A topic that locals are very passionate about sharing.

Tracy Carmen Watkin

WELCOME TO
> TOURIST

Barcelona
Spain

Tracy Carmen Watkin

INTRODUCTION

They should tell you when you're born: have a suitcase heart, be ready to travel.
–Gabrielle Zevin

Of the countless 'Barcelona trip planning' emails I've exchanged with people over the years, the common response I've received once they are boarding the plane back home is, "I wish I'd had more time to just wander the streets". This is typically my strongest suggestion when helping them plan. Of course there are amazing sights, museums and exhibitions to see, but the biggest mistake one can make, is to over plan their trip to Barcelona. This city is so vibrant and the culture so rich; this city respects 'siesta' and long, two-hour lunches. There is nothing fast-paced about the life here, so if you truly want to experience Barcelona like a local, slow down. Any time of year is a good time to visit Barcelona, but from my experience, Spring (April and May) and Fall (September and October) tend to be the least expensive times to travel and have the mildest weather.

Barcelona Climate

	High	Low
January	59	48
February	59	47
March	63	50
April	67	55
May	73	60
June	80	68
July	84	73
August	85	74
September	79	69
October	73	62
November	65	54
December	60	49

GreaterThanaTourist.com

Temperatures are in Fahrenheit degrees.
Source: NOAA

1. WANDER THROUGH EL BORN

I begin here because this little neighborhood is where I found 'home' in Barcelona. El Born is one of four neighborhoods in Ciutat Vella (translation: Old City). Here you will find independent boutique clothing shops, upscale cocktail bars, and restaurants of local cuisine. During warm months, you can sit out at a restaurant terrace and enjoy the street performers who go terrace to terrace showing off their talents. Don't forget to give them some small change if you enjoyed their show!

Take a stroll down Passeig del Born, duck into Hoffman bakery for a decadent croissant and find a bench to enjoy savoring the snack and the ambiance. This is a perfect place to watch the world go by.

2. DUCK INTO THE CULTURAL AND MEMORIAL CENTER

The Centre de Cultura I Memòria located in El Born is a great place to learning about the culture and history of the old city. In the late 1800s, this building housed the old market. It was only during a renovation of the space in 1979 that they found ruins dating back to the 1700s below the structure. In 1994 they began excavations, and in 2013 the space was re-opened as El Born Centre Cultural. There is no entrance fee to the building; although, there are exhibitions you can pay to visit here.

The large open space makes it easy to view the ruins below, and I recommend you stroll through the building, pausing to read the historical plaques and taking a moment to think about what it must have been like to be living during that time. There is a small bookstore/gift shop here where you can pick up a souvenir to remember your visit and support the center.

3. STROLL THROUGH THE PARK

At the edge of Ciutat Vella lies a vast green space known as Parc de la Ciutadella. Although there are many attractions here: a zoo, museums, the Catalan parliament building…etc., I recommend a leisurely stroll through the park beginning at the entrance off of Carrer Princesa. As you walk through the gates, you will pass a large castle-like building on the left, the Castell dels Tres Dragons (Castle of the Three Dragons) which is an example of early Modernism which housed the Zoological museum. A few more steps and you come to a wide gravel path, look left and you will see the Arc de Triomf. Continue on to one of the smaller dirt paths and you will come to an opening where you will find a beautiful, monumental waterfall. Stop here for a photo, or sit at the outdoor café to take in the sight for just a little while longer.

As you leave the waterfall, take a right and you will pass by a large stone sculpture of a mammoth, continue on and you will see a lake to your right. As you circle the lake, you will find an area of rowboats for hourly rent. Next, you might want to find a grassy spot to sit and enjoy the warm sunshine. Don't forget to pack a snack and beverage, this is the perfect place to picnic.

4. BARCELONA BY FOOT

If you are already an avid walker and outdoors person, you will be pleased to find that Barcelona is very do-able by foot. While Barcelona boasts one of the best metro systems in Europe, it isn't always necessary to take transportation. If you're willing to plan a little extra time to get to your destination, your travel on foot will certainly help you see more of the city. If you're not in a hurry, pop into an interesting-looking café or bar on the way.

5. VERMUT LIKE A LOCAL

Traditionally on Sundays, Catalans gather with friends and/or family before lunch to 'have a Vermut' (Vermouth). This sweet, wine-like beverage can be served with or without ice and often accompanied by a squirt of seltzer water, an olive, and possibly an orange rind. Many bodegas and bars in Barcelona serve their very own homemade version of this drink.

If you are in Barcelona on a Sunday, don't miss out on this cultural tradition. Historically after mass and before lunch (between the hours of about 12-2), you would see local Catalans having a Vermut and a snack to prepare their stomachs for their big lunch.

6. GO TOUCH THE OLD ROMAN WALL

In Ciutat Vella (the Old City), just across Via Laietana from el Born, you will find the Gothic quarter. The Gothic quarter houses the oldest parts of the city of Barcelona, including the old Roman wall that encircled the entire old city, and part of the original aqueduct. If you walk around the areas of the wall into the Barcelona Cathedral plaza, you will find signage that dates the wall back to the 4th century. In this plaza, you will also find a bronze monument that reads: Barcino, which is the name of the original city. Take a picture next to the Barcino sign, and touch the old wall where it connects to the bridge (the entrance to the old city).

7. EAT TAPAS

You can find Tapas in just about every restaurant in Barcelona. A word of advice: don't eat at places where there are pictures of the food on the outside of the restaurant. These are almost always tourist traps and can be disappointing. There are amazing restaurants in Barcelona and really terrible ones. If you are looking for authentic Tapas, I suggest heading into Barceloneta. Barceloneta is the third neighborhood in Ciutat Vella (El Born and the Gothic Quarter being the first two I've mentioned). Barceloneta is the old fishing village and is located right next to the sea.

Some of the best authentic Tapas restaurants are here. My two favorites are: Jai-ca and Vaso de Oro. Located on Carrer Ginebra, Jai-ca has an impressive selection of Tapas. The first time I visited this restaurant, I asked for a menu and the waiter shrugged his shoulders and said 'look around at what other people have and order what you see'. They've since put together a menu to help with ordering confusion. Everything here is tasty, and they serve most common Tapas: Patatas Bravas (fried, diced potatoes with 'bravas sauce'), Pan con Tomate (bread with tomato rubbed on it and salted), Pimientos de Padron (small, fried green peppers), Calamares (deep-fried squid). If you're brave, you might try the Pulpo (octopus), Chipirones (deep-fried baby squid or cuttlefish), or Callos (Spanish-style Tripe).

Just a block and a half away, on Carrer de Balboa, you will find Vaso de Oro. Here, the ambiance is a little different and the restaurant is quite small. When you enter, you are directly in front of the bar, which stretches the length of the restaurant. Behind the bar, the bartenders are hard at work calling out orders to each other, making the food, and pouring drinks; it is obvious they love what they do. If you are lucky enough to get a seat at the bar or one of the few tables they have, you are in for a treat!

My favorite thing to eat here is the Pepito, which is a high-quality cut of steak lightly salted and cooked on the grill in a little bit of olive oil and served on a toasted bun. There is nothing like it! Vaso de Oro makes their own beer. They offer a light beer or a dark beer, or you can get 'una mezcla', a mix of the two. If you're a fan of cheese, order the Manchego, it comes with salted almonds. Que aproveche!

8. TAKE A DIP IN THE MED

Between about late May and late October, you will find the beaches crowded with people. If you've never dipped a toe in the Mediterranean Sea before, now is your opportunity. Barcelona is a coastal city, which makes swimming in the Med very easy. The water during the Summer and Fall is typically warm and comfortable for a dip. Join the thousands of beach-goers and head down to the playa for an afternoon. Bring your lunch with you for a beach picnic, or visit one of the 'chiringuitos' (beach bars) that line the beach. Play a pick-up game of volleyball at one of the many courts on the beach, or learn petanca from a local.

A couple beach tips: the farther south you are on the beach (closer to the W hotel), the cleaner the beach is and the leass clothing worn. Also, always keep an eye on your belongings; there are frequent accounts of opportunistic theft here. Bring as little as possible with you to the beach to avoid having to worry about this, or go with a group and take turns swimming so someone can be responsible for your group's things.

9. ENJOY PINTXOS ON CARRER DE BLAI

In the neighborhood of Poble-Sec, there is a street called 'Carrer de Blai', which is well known for its string of Pintxo bars. A pintxo is a small finger-food typically pierced with a toothpick. They usually consist of a base of a slice of baguette with some sort of topping. For example, one pintxo might be a slice of baguette, topped with a slice of goat cheese, and honey and balsamic vinegar drizzled on top with a toothpick in the center. They can be savory or sweet.

There are infinite creative options, which is why moving from restaurant to restaurant is ideal. This is akin to a sport; choosing a restaurant, finding space at the bar, picking your favorite pintxos, ordering a beverage to accompany them, balancing your plate and glass while conversing with friends, and then counting up your toothpicks to pay at the end. Then on to the next bar where it starts all over again.

10. SPEND SOME TIME ON MONTJUÏC

Montjuïc is a large hill in Barcelona overlooking the port. Translated often to 'Mount of the Jews', there is documentation that a Jewish gravesite was found here. Nowadays, this hill is bustling with tourists and locals as there are many activities to participate in here. If you are an athletic person who enjoys exercise on your travels, you might enjoy a run or walk up this hill. Join the many locals who use this historic landmark to stay in shape.

No need to worry if you prefer to take it easy, you can ride the funicular or gondola up to the top and check out the amazing views along the way. Once at the top, you can check out the old castle, which dates back to 1640 and was first used as a military fortress. Don't forget your camera on this excursion, there are multiple photo opportunities along the way.

11. CHECK OUT THE OPEN AIR FILM FESTIVAL

If you happen to be in Barcelona during the summer, the Montjuïc film festival is a must! This festival runs from late June to August atop this big hill, and the movies are projected onto the side of the castle wall! Be sure to research ahead of time, as the popular movies tend to sell out fast. There are 2-3 movies each week from all over the globe. All movies have Spanish and/or Catalan subtitles; however, there are many American and English films available throughout the summer.

Arrive early to the castle as seating is 'first come first served' and don't forget your picnic blankets, food, and wine. Before each film, you will have the pleasure of enjoying a musical performance while you picnic. This is one attraction you won't want to miss!

12. GO SEE SOME ART

On the north-west side of Montjuïc sits the National Art Museum of Catalunya. Here, you can

25

see works of art from the early Middle Ages to the 20th century. The museum is well laid out with large sections and rooms for each period. This museum is especially known for its Romanesque and Gothic art.

The view from the base of the museum is impressive; it is situated on the hill overlooking Plaza Espanya. Make sure to stop for a beverage at the outdoor café, and relax in one of the comfy chairs after being on your feet for so long. Once you've had a chance to rest, you will want to walk slowly down the hill, pausing to take photos of the grand steps and building on your way down.

13. LEARN MORE ABOUT CATALUNYA

It was a conscious decision to name this book Barcelona, Catalunya, Spain. Many Catalan people don't consider themselves 'Spanish'. There is a long history here of oppression and struggle for independence. Before moving to Barcelona, I read a lot about the history of Spain and Catalunya. After moving to Barcelona, I spent several hours at the Catalan History Museum located in Barceloneta. This museum has information about the history of Catalunya from the Stone Age to present day.

I highly recommend a visit to this museum, but if you are on a short visit to Barcelona, at the very least strike up a conversation with a local Catalan and ask them a bit about the history. Most Catalans are eager to share the history of their land and people.

14. GAWK AT GAUDÍ'S ARCHITECTURE

Barcelona and the famous architect Antoni Gaudí go hand in hand. You will find his work all over this city, from the expansive Parc Güell, to the well-known La Sagrada Familia, his impressive one-of-a-kind style of modernist art can't be missed. If you have the time and budget, tours of both of these works are well worth it. If you can only choose one, most locals will tell you that a visit to La Sagrada Familia is a good way to spend a few hours. If your trip is really short on time, you can get a good idea of Gaudí's work by taking a walk up Passeig de Gràcia from Plaza Catalunya. Here you will find two of Gaudí's buildings: Casa Batlló and La Pedrera.

15. SHOP OFF THE BEATEN PATH

El Raval is the fourth neighborhood that makes up Ciutat Vella. It is most known for its diverse and multi-cultural population. In the winding streets of el Raval, you can find a variety of vintage and vinyl shops. These quirky vintage shops all have something unique and different about them. One has a bar in the back near the dressing rooms, another sells their clothes per kilo. Most of these shops are located on Carrer de Tallers and Carrer de la Riera Baixa, but don't limit yourself to just those streets if you are a vintage shopper.

All throughout el Raval you will find shops that carry new and used vinyl records. I've been successful in finding some amazing deals on records of American artists which were passed over by locals who were looking for something different.

16. ENJOY SOME GOOD COFFEE

I thought that moving to Barcelona automatically meant I would be drinking good coffee. I'm not sure where I came up with this logic, but it failed me. Luckily, there are specialty coffee shops popping up all around the city. There are three that I am particularly fond of and if you get a chance, stop into one of them for a quality cup of coffee or a specialty drink, and consider taking home some beans for when you're feeling nostalgic about your visit to Barcelona.

Cafés el Magnífico is located in el Born on Carrer de l'Argenteria, this family business has been roasting and brewing coffee in the neighborhood for three generations. Magnífico has a large selection of beans available for purchase and they also hold 'coffee tastings'. In the heat of the summer, I suggest trying their Shakerato. Here, you will always be greeted with a friendly smile.

Also in el Born you will find Nømad Coffee, which is a small café located on Passatge de Sert. Each cup they brew feels unique and special; coffee is always made with passion here. Note that this coffee 'lab' is for connoisseurs only--you will not find sugar here.

Located in the Gothic Quarter on Carrer de l'Arc de Sant Ramon del Call is Satan's Coffee Corner. Here you will find more than just coffee; baked goods, cold-pressed juices, chia pudding, sandwiches, and salads make their menu more extensive than others. You can take the time to sit and read the paper or one of the many magazines lying around.

Each of these cafés has multiple locations Visit their official websites for more information.

17. TAKE A SIESTA

My first several months living in Barcelona, I wasn't exactly sure what to do with my day between the hours of 2pm-5pm. Everything, and I mean everything besides restaurants was closed. Coming from fast-paced and super-productive America, I was unable to wind down in the middle of the day. Then the summer came, and without air conditioning in the sticky humidity, the only way to stop sweating was to lie still. Apparently siesta began as a way for farmers to escape the heat of the day, and today, shops, churches, museums, and some schools still implement it. Mediterranean culture favors long lunches--often with wine or beer--and a short siesta is a great way to beat the midday drowsiness. So head out on your adventures, but be sure to return to your hotel or room for a short siesta to restore your energy.

18. BROWSE THE MARKET

Each neighborhood has their own Mercat (Market) where locals will go at least weekly to shop for meat, cheese, fruit, and vegetables for their families. The brilliant colors, variety, and strange smells are unlike anything I had experienced before. If you are staying in the city center, check out La Boqueria located on La Rambla. Local tip: be sure to head towards the back of the market if you decide to purchase anything, the front stalls tend to be more touristy and have higher prices.

I also recommend you visit Mercat de Santa Caterina located in el Born. This newer market is a bit more spacious than La Boqueria and much less touristy. There are often wine and food-tasting events just out front of this market, and if you happen to be visiting when one of these is going on, you're in for a treat.

19. GET TO AND FROM THE AIRPORT

Transportation in Barcelona is inexpensive and easy. There is an official airport bus (aerobus) from both terminal 1 and terminal 2 that goes straight to the city center. The bus runs frequently, every 5 or 10 minutes depending on the terminal, and the journey is only 35 minutes long. The most central stops are Plaza Espanya, Plaza Universitat, and Plaza Catalunya. If your travel to and from the airport is within 2 weeks, be sure to ask for 'ida y vuelta' (a return ticket) for a discounted price.

If you are staying a bit outside the center, there is also a train and metro option for airport travel. Be sure to do your research on this ahead of time. You can always rely on taxis as well if you are in a hurry or have a lot of luggage with you.

20. TALK LIKE A LOCAL

Did you know that Catalunya has its very own language? While there are similarities between Catalan and Spanish, some would say it's closer to French or Portuguese. In Barcelona, you can get by in

English and some Spanish, but if you want to impress the Catalan people and not stand out as a tourist, you might want to learn a few phrases. When greeting someone in the morning, you would say: bon dia, to greet someone in the afternoon: bona tarda. Afternoon in Spain lasts until at least 7 pm or 8 pm. To say goodbye when leaving a shop or restaurant, you would say: adéu, and if you think you might be seeing them again, you could say: fins aviat.

21. SPEND SOME TIME IN GRÀCIA

Gràcia is a neighborhood just outside of the city center that has, for the most part, remained pretty local. This part of Barcelona is vibrant, full of amazing shops and restaurants but also has the feel of a small village. There are several large plazas full of restaurant terraces, and many activities take place in these plazas throughout the year. Every neighborhood and village in Catalunya has a yearly festival. Gràcia's festival is one of the best and biggest in Barcelona. Each August, the locals living in Gràcia spend weeks decorating their street before the week-long festival. They are in fierce competition, and the entire neighborhood is transformed into a magical wonderland. The theme changes with each year, and it is clear that this neighborhood houses many talented artists. If you happen to be in Barcelona in August, don't miss this celebration!

22. WATCH A HUMAN TOWER COMPETITION

Another aspect of the rich culture of Catalunya is their sport of human towers. Dating back to the 18th century, this competition has grown and spread to all of Catalunya. The sport is known as 'Castellers' – Castell in Catalan translates to Castle and includes men, women, and children. This is quite a serious sport here and the competitions are exciting and terrifying to watch. The towers are made up of people, and--using precise technique--they form a strong base as other members begin standing on each other's shoulders to form the trunk. For the finale, the smallest of the group climbs to the top and raises their hand, signifying the completion of their tower. Then they uniformly scramble down each other's backs and shoulders to the bottom.

The Casteller's season runs from June to November, you can find a schedule online. Most of the large festivals in Catalunya will have a performance, but it is definitely worth seeking out if you are not in Barcelona during one of these festivals. If you make friends with a local who is on a Castell team, ask to attend a practice, you may even get to participate!

23. GO CHEER ON BARÇA IN A LOCAL BAR

Fútbol (soccer) is an important part of Spanish culture, and Barcelona's team: FC Barcelona, is one of the best in the world. Going to the stadium, Camp Nou, to watch a match can be an exciting activity, but the camaraderie of a bar often tops it. A 'Penya' is the name for an official bar that supports Barça and each neighborhood across the city has at least one. If you can't find a Penya, look for a small bar filled with locals and enjoy watching top quality fútbol. It's acceptable to watch the entire match and only order 1 or 2 drinks.

24. THE SWEETER SIDE OF BARCELONA

If you have a sweet tooth, you are in the right place. Desserts, or 'Postres', are abundant here and an important part of the Catalan cuisine. Many restaurants make their sweets in-house and each homemade recipe will have its own unique flair. Some of the local desserts I recommend trying:

Crema Catalana – This crème-brulée-like dessert is served in a terracotta dish called a cazuela. It has similar ingredients to the French custard counterpart with the addition of cinnamon and often times orange peel for flavoring.

Mel i Mato – Translated Honey and Mato, which is a fresh cow or goat cheese with no salt added, similar to ricotta. The honey is drizzled on top of the cheese, and I've seen variations with caramelized honey or garnished with nuts.

25. MENÚ DEL DÍA: HOW TO LUNCH

One of the things I love most about Barcelona is lunch. It is the largest meal in the Spanish culture, and locals don't usually sit down for the meal before 2 pm. Most restaurants offer what is called a Menú del Día (daily menu), which is fixed price with a few options to choose from. It typically starts off with a soup, salad, or pasta and then the main course of fish or meat (many restaurants also have a vegetarian option) and lastly, a dessert of your choice. The menu almost always includes bread for the table and a beverage; if you're not a fan of sweets, you can ask your server to bring you a coffee in place of the dessert.

Another tip: If you order a coffee as well as dessert, it will be served after. If you'd like your coffee with your dessert, make sure to mention this to your server.

26. VISIT A PALACE OF MUSIC

Palau de la Musica is a modernist palace for musical performances built between 1905-1908. It sits on the edge of several different neighborhoods in Ciutat Vella and is a grand and colorful sight. If you want to experience a concert in this beautiful building, check out their website for tickets and information. When you pass by the front of the building, you will notice two small and detailed ticket windows that are still in use today. For a less expensive option, go around the back of the building where you will enter into a large open room with ornate modernist details and a bar in the middle of the room. You don't have to have a concert ticket to sit and have a beverage or small snack and take in the ambiance. Don't forget to make your way to the elegant restrooms before you leave.

27. MEDITATE INSIDE SANTA MARIA DEL MAR

Located in the heart of el Born is Santa Maria del Mar, a little church with a lot of history. This church was constructed from 1329 to 1384, commissioned, paid for, and built by the local community in just over 50 years. During this time, churches and cathedrals took at least a century to complete, because of the short time period for construction, Santa Maria del Mar remains one of the strongest and purest examples of Catalan Gothic architecture. It has survived earthquakes and fires; you can read all about the history inside the church, or pay for a guided tour for more information.

I suggest arriving early before a service with a journal and take a seat for a while. Enjoy the beauty of this church, the slightly charred ceiling, the intricate rose window, the smell of candles burning. Here would be a good time to sit and write about your trip, or just meditate on the moment and the amazing history you are in the midst of.

28. BARTER FOR A TREASURE AT ENCANTS

Els Encants is the largest flea market in Barcelona and one of the oldest in Europe, dating back to the 14th century. In 2013, the market moved to a new, shiny building where it is contained but still has the same open-air feel to it. Here you can wander the aisles and feast your eyes on many old trinkets and treasures. If you are willing to get up close and personal and rummage around through another man's trash, you very well could walk away with your very own treasure.

29. FEEL DEEPLY FOR THE LOCALS

While wandering through the gothic quarter, make a point to seek out Plaça de Sant Felip Neri. When not full of children from the school here, this plaza can be one of the most romantic and tranquil spots in all of Barcelona, but don't let that fool you. If you walk up close to the walls, you can touch the marks and scars of bombs. During the Civil War, Franco's air force dropped bombs here killing 42 people, most of them children who were taking shelter inside. Marking this memory is a plaque, which reads: In memory of the victims of the bombing of Sant Felip Neri. Here died 42 people – the majority children – due to the actions of Franco's air force on the 30th of January 1938.

30. JOIN THE LATE NIGHT CROWD

El Raval neighborhood has so much going on. After a day of vintage shopping and browsing for vinyl albums here, join the crowd of late-nighters on one of the trendiest streets in Barcelona, Carrer de Joaquín Costa. Here you will find everything from posh-hipster bars like 33/45 or Betty Ford, to historic bars like Almirall, which remains unchanged in its original Catalan modernist décor from the 19th century. Also lining Joaquín Costa is Bar Olímpic known for its reasonable prices and frozen-in-time interior as well as many other hip and interesting bars--each with their own decorative niche.

'Late night' in Barcelona is considered anything after midnight. On a typical weekend night, you will find locals sitting down to dinner around 10 pm and then heading out to bars after midnight. If you are someone who enjoys going out to dance clubs, expect to begin your night out dancing around 1 or 2am. These clubs close around 5 or 6 am, and bars close around 3 am.

31. SEE A CONCERT

If you are a lover of music, you will be delighted to know that Barcelona has many concert venues to choose from. Go online before your trip to see if any of these concert halls are featuring artists that you are interested in seeing.

Razzmatazz features 5 different rooms or concert halls and holds several concerts each week (often big-name/popular artists). In addition to concerts, this club also has regular DJ sessions.

Jamboree is an underground cave-like space located in the famous Plaça Reial featuring well-known jazz artists in the evening and then transforms into a hip-hop club at night.

Teatre Liceu is an opera house located on La Rambla. This beautiful hall opened in 1847 and, after a tragic fire in 1994, was rebuilt with state of the art equipment and reopened in 1999. It is one of the biggest opera houses in the world and holds modern and classical opera performances as well as other performances. They also offer daily tours of the magnificent building.

Sala Apolo is possibly Barcelona's most popular venue, featuring weekly concerts as well as DJ club nights. The live music here ranges from Rockabilly to

Big Band Jazz including pop and rock and everything in between.

32. DISCOVER A LOCAL SECRET

Antic Teatre is one of those places you find out about because a friend brought you there, it is almost impossible to stumble upon otherwise. Set on a small street in el Born, Antic Teatre is an independent theater and cultural center, which features artistic performances of up and coming local artists.

Well-known for its large open-air patio and terrace, there is something tranquil and special here. When the sun goes down, the lights hanging from the large fig tree in the middle of the patio give a magical feeling to the space. It is a popular spot among locals, so you may have to wait for a table, but it's worth it. There are no servers, so you must go get your own drink and snacks at the bar inside. This charming secret is one you won't want to miss.

33. KNOWING HOW TO TIP

Feel free to do what is most comfortable for you, but know that the salary of the individual in Barcelona does not rely on receiving tips. People are paid a fair wage for service jobs and tipping large amounts is not very common by locals. If you would like to leave something for your dining experience, a rule of thumb is to just round up. If your lunch came to €14.10, it's okay to leave €15. This is the same with taxi rides as well. In restaurants where you pay by card, there is not a custom of being able to write a tip on the receipt after you pay. If you have change on you, and you enjoyed your dining experience, feel free to leave it.

34. BARCELONA BY SEASON

Catalans are great at celebrating. Here you will find festivals and holidays by month and season. There is always something going on in Barcelona, no matter when you visit.

January

If you happen to be in Barcelona over New Year's Eve, be sure to stop by a grocery store to buy 12 grapes. At each chime of the clock at midnight, eat a grape. If you are able to do all 12 before the last chime, it is said that you will have good luck for the year.

Catalan children receive gifts on January 6th 'Kings Day' brought to them by the Magos (wise men) which parade through Barcelona on the 5th of January from the port in a spectacular event fun for all ages.

February - March

Carnival is a joyful time where young and old can dress up and participate in the many parades and events. The coastal town of Sitges, just south of Barcelona, is well-known for its Carnival party.

Don't miss out on attending a Calçotada (Catalan winter barbeque) during the late winter. Calçots are leek-like vegetables, which are grilled over an open flame. They are served on roof tiles; you pull off the outer charred layer, dip it into a red sauce called Romesco, tilt back your head, and dangle it into your mouth. Don't fill up too much on calçots, because the second course is a large plate of various meats often accompanied by white beans.

April

April 23rd is Sant Jordi, which is a festival of love where locals exchange roses and books with each other. (I encourage you to research more about this lovely cultural holiday).

June

June 23$^{rd-24th}$ is one of the biggest Catalan holidays, Sant Joan. Often described as the 'nit de foc' (night of fire), locals celebrate in the streets and on the beach with music, fireworks, and bonfires until the early hours of the morning.

August

The Festa Major de Gracìa is a week-long celebration in the month of August. This neighborhood decorates the streets transforming them into a fantasy land. There are concerts, food, and drink all week long.

September

La Diada, on September 11th is the national day of Catalunya. It is a day-long celebration commemorating the 14-month siege of Catalunya which ultimately ended in surrender to the Spanish crown. It is a day of remembrance and celebration of culture, language, and tradition.

La Mercè celebrates the patron saint of Barcelona. It is a week-long citywide festival with concerts, parades, and fire. It is the main festival in Barcelona and is quite spectacular.

December

The Christmas markets begin to open and the streets are decorated with lights marking the beginning of the Christmas season.

35. DRESS THE PART

Barcelona is not like Paris or New York, you will not notice name brands walking around or a specific fashion style. The one thing I've learned about living in Barcelona is that basically anything goes. It is a slow, casual lifestyle, which is also reflected in the clothing the locals wear. They tend to dress sharp, but relaxed. I have sat at some of the most elegant restaurants in Barcelona, and looking around, there are still many wearing jeans and/or sweatshirts. Yes, you can dress up, but you definitely don't have to.

While Barcelona is a very casually dressed city, you won't find many locals in flip-flops or shorts unless it's summer. The locals here stick to season-appropriate wear and frown on those who dress outside the season. For instance, if you are from a cold and snowy climate, the winter in Barcelona may feel very mild to you, but if you leave your lodging in shorts and a t-shirt, be prepared to get many odd looks.

You will also notice that locals wear comfortable and practical shoes. Much of the ground is cobblestone and makes walking in heels very difficult. Save the heels for home or bring only one pair for a special night out.

Please do your research if you are going to a nightclub, many do have simple 'dress codes' to follow.

36. STAY SAFE

I've lived in Barcelona for over 6 years and feel that it is a very safe city. Partly due to the late nightlife here, there are almost always other people out and the streets are lit all night long. The thing to be the most aware of in Barcelona is theft. I have heard countless stories of people getting their stuff stolen while at the beach, or at a restaurant, or even just walking around town. These thefts have one thing in common: they are opportunistic.

Make sure you wear a purse or bag that crosses over your chest. When you are at a restaurant, you need to be holding all of your items on your lap.

Especially sitting out on a restaurant terrace, you cannot leave your purse or bag on a free chair at your table. I have had to get used to wearing my purse while dining and now, even when visiting relatives in the U.S., I find myself holding my items close to my body out of habit.

When retrieving money from your purse or wallet, only take out what you need in that moment. Keep your wallet in your front pocket instead of your back pocket. Leave your expensive jewelry at home. I mentioned this in an earlier post, but if you decide to take a swim while at the beach, ask someone to watch your items or take turns with the people in your group. Enjoy this wonderful city, but keep your belongings in mind.

37. JAMÓN JAMÓN JAMÓN

Catalans eat a lot of pork. It is the most important meat in Catalan cuisine and available in just about any form you can think of. Eating so much pork was an adjustment for me when I moved to Barcelona. Americans eat far more beef than pork, and this was something I had to get used to. Early on, I went to watch a friend play in a fútbol match and ordered a hamburger at the concessions stand. I wasn't expecting an actual 'ham' burger. That was the moment I realized how seriously Catalans took their pork consumption.

Be sure to try Jamón Ibérico, which is a cured ham popular in most restaurants and grocery stores. The pigs are fed acorns and olives, which give the meat a rich, nutty flavor. Another popular pork item to try is embutidos, which are cured, dried sausages such as choriço or fuet. Possibly the most common way to eat pork here is in the form of Butifarra, which is ground pork-meat flavored with spices and stuffed into natural casings. They are then grilled and served as an appetizer or alongside white beans.

Many of the cured meats are available in local grocery stores. This is a great gift to bring back to friends and family, give them a taste of Catalunya without breaking the bank.

38. TASTE THE LOCAL OLIVE OIL

The Mediterranean is well-known for its foods, and high on that list is olive oil. The Romans called olive oil 'liquid gold' and even used it to bathe. Spain happens to be the biggest producer of olive oil so while you are here, taste some varieties of olives and oil and bring some back for your friends and family. Olive oil is an essential part of the Spanish diet, and locals buy it in jugs of 3+ liters.

While you may not be able to fit 3 liters of olive oil into your suitcase to bring back home, there are many local shops where you can find olive oil products in small bottles. In el Born, there is a shop called La Chinata that has olive oil in many different forms: lip balm, soap, lotion, and different flavored oils. They even have a section where you can taste oil made from different varieties of olives.

39. LEARN ABOUT PICASSO

El Born is home to the world-famous Picasso Museum. The only museum of Picasso's work to be opened during his life, this building houses much of his earlier and later work, not the typical paintings you know him by. Picasso lived with his family in Barcelona before moving to France and although born in Málaga, the south of Spain, when his longtime friend Jaume Sabartés proposed the idea of opening the museum in Málaga, Picasso suggested Barcelona instead noting that it would be more appropriate. The museum opened in 1963, just 10 years before Pablo Picasso would die. The collection has grown much over the years as friends and family members of Picasso have made donations.

40. HIKE IN THE HILLS JUST BEYOND THE CITY

Just outside of Barcelona lies a small mountain range that separates the city from the valley. Spanning almost 20,000 acres, this large park has many trails winding through it. The highest point reaches almost 1700 feet with a spectacular view of the entire city and the sea. If you are an outdoorsy person, this is a great way to spend a few hours. Pack a picnic, wear good walking shoes, and head out to the nearest train station. Just a mere 20-minute train ride from Plaza Catalunya, you can exit Baixador de Vallvidrera and start your adventure from there.

Tip: following the path from the train stop, you will pass by a visitors center where you can find maps and other information for your hike.

41. VISIT A SPANISH WINE REGION

Just one hour south of Barcelona is the Penedès wine region. Known for its sparkling white (cava) and rose wines, they also feature exquisite reds as well. If you have the time, I'd highly recommend an overnight trip to the region. There are many Bed and Breakfast style lodgings, and some fantastic restaurants to eat at. If you are short on time, world-famous Freixenet Cava Cellars features a comprehensive guided tour and tasting. You can buy the train ticket combined with the guided tour and tasting on the Freixenet website. Make sure to book in advance and select your preferred language for the tour.

42. TRAVEL TO A BETTER BEACH

While Barcelona has its own beach, the Catalan coastline has so much more to offer. If you're interested in getting out of the city for a few hours, traveling one to two hours north or south by train can make all the difference in your beach experience. I suggest taking the train north to Sant Pol de Mar where you won't have to share the beach with many tourists. When you leave the train, there is a beautiful beach in front of you, but if you are willing to walk a little to the left (facing the water), you will find smaller beaches with beautiful, clear water. The town of Sant Pol is charming as well, however if you are strolling the streets around siesta, it might feel like a ghost town.

Another option is to take the train south and explore Sitges, which is a delightful beach town with a beautiful historic center. Known for its festivals and nightlife scene, there are also many notable restaurants to choose from here. I recommend taking a walk along the seafront promenade and exploring the old town.

43. TAKE A TRAIN TO GIRONA

If you are looking to get out of Barcelona for the day, Girona is a beautiful city to visit. Just under an hour by train, there is so much to see here. Known for its old quarter (Barri Vell) and medieval architecture, you can get wonderfully lost roaming the streets. A canal runs through the town separating the colorful buildings and you can tour the old Arab baths located in the center of town, or walk the grand stone staircase to the cathedral at the top of the hill. There is also a Jewish museum, film museum, and an archaeology museum located in Girona. There is so much history to learn about in this small, enchanting city.

44. SUNDAY IN BARCELONA

On Sundays in Barcelona, most shops are closed. If you are hoping to shop for clothing or gifts, or if you need to go to a grocery store to buy food, plan to do it on another day. Restaurants are open and this is a great day to go out for a meal. The concept of Sunday brunch is new to Barcelona and you will find many restaurants offering brunch menus (especially in the neighborhood of l'Eixample).

Sundays are excellent museum days. Check online before your trip to see if any of the museums you are interested in are offering free days while you are visiting. Many free days fall on Sundays, and this is something to take advantage of. I recommend looking into the Barcelona History Museum, Catalan History

Museum, or the Picasso Museum. Another special thing about being in Barcelona on a Sunday is that many of the cathedrals charge for entrance throughout the week, but if you go on Sunday around the time of Sunday Mass, you can often enter free of charge. Just remember to be respectful as many locals are worshipping here.

45. LODGING TIPS

I highly recommend staying in the city center, it makes seeing the sights and getting a feel for the city and its heartbeat easier. There are many hotels and hostels to choose from in el Born, el Gotico, and l'Eixample. If you are on a tighter budget and decide to look to rent a flat through a vacation rental company such as, Airbnb, please try to rent one that is legally registered with the city. There are a lot of problems with tourist flats within the city, and disrespectful lodgers. Keep in mind that if you do stay in a rented flat, the neighbors around you are living their normal daily lives.

One thing to be aware of is that many buildings do not have elevators in them. If you are in need of one, make sure you ask the hotel, hostel, or apartment manager before booking. Also in Spain, if something is listed as 1st floor, it is not ground level. The way floors are designed varies between buildings, but as an example, there is often: 'planta baja' which houses the ground floor shop or restaurant, next would be 'entresuelo' which literally translates to 'in-between floor', often a storage room. Above that is 'principal', and finally the actual numbering of floors would begin with primero – 1st floor, Segundo – 2nd floor, and so on all the way up to 'ático' which is the top floor.

46. GET ON SPANISH TIME

One thing I've learned while living in Spain is that times differ from the U.S. in many ways. One example of this is meal times. Here, the locals traditionally eat more meals daily. One might have a piece of toast before heading to work, and around 10 am take another break for a coffee and bocadillo (baguette sandwich). Lunch isn't until 2 pm and can last for several hours. If there are children in the household, they might eat a snack after work/school around 5 pm, which is called 'merienda'. And lastly, dinner is served around 9 pm. If this is your first time in Europe, getting used to the later nights might be hard for you, as many restaurants don't open for dinner before 8:30/9 pm.

47. BARCELONA BUS TOURS

Having lived in Barcelona for several years, I still highly recommend the bus tour. It gives a great overview of the city and is a good way to begin your adventure. You can save your legs for your first day by riding atop a bus and recover from jet lag while planning out what you want to see and do. If you've never been to Barcelona, this is a good way to familiarize yourself with the layout of the city.

The bus ticket also doubles as public transport, as it stops in many popular areas of the city. The tickets can be bought for one or two days and I would suggest riding at least one route all the way around, and then the second time around, use it to hop on and hop off at attractions you want to see. The maps that come with the bus tours are also especially helpful to use during your visit.

You can go online before your trip and buy tickets for this tour, or there is a kiosk in Plaza Catalunya where you can purchase tickets. Be prepared to wait in line if you don't buy them in advance.

48. EXPLORE THE JEWISH QUARTER

Tucked into the winding streets of the Gothic Quarter, you will find El Call – the Jewish quarter of Barcelona. Practically hidden here, is a Jewish synagogue where Jewish families gathered together to learn and worship as early as the 14th century. Duck into the synagogue and you will find a small museum where you can pay a fee to sit for a historical presentation and see many old artifacts. This structure is said to have been in existence since the 5th century, due to its Roman foundations, and this synagogue is thought to be the oldest in Europe.

After leaving the museum, take some time to wander these narrow streets. Nearby is a plaza with a few cafés and restaurants. Stop into Caj Chai for a warm spicy chai tea, or taste some local wines and tapas next door at Zona d'Ombra. You will also find Satan's Coffee Corner here with some of the best coffee in all of Barcelona.

49. MAKE THE PILGRIMAGE TO MONTSERRAT

Maybe you've heard of Montserrat, the strange looking mountain range just outside of Barcelona. Montserrat, meaning serrated mountain, is just that-- its jagged peaks draw tourists from all over. High up on this mountain sits a Benedictine Abbey featuring a statue of the Virgin of Monserrat, Mary and child. Many make the pilgrimage from afar to see this statue, which, with time has darkened creating what is now referred to as the 'black Madonna'. You will most likely have to wait in a long line to see her, but the visit is free of charge. As you move through the line into the basilica, be sure to take in the sights including the chapels leading to the Madonna statue.

There is more to see atop this mountain: an art museum, gift shop, and for the more adventurous, hiking and climbing. Be sure to check the timetables for the train to the foot of the mountain. From there you will have to take either the cable car or cremallera up the mountain. The cremallera and cable car don't run very late into the evening, it is good to know the timetables as you don't want to be stranded up on this mountain by accident.

50. JUST GO GET LOST

As I mentioned in my introduction, the majority of the people I help plan trips for comment that they didn't just wander enough. There is so much to see of Barcelona, so many sights, museums, parks, so many restaurants to eat at and cathedrals to walk through. I can guarantee that if you leave your room with no scheduled plan, and wander aimlessly with no direction in mind, and eventually find your way back home, that will be the most memorable day of your trip.

Tracy Carmen Watkin

TOP REASONS TO BOOK THIS TRIP

Culture and History: The vibrant Catalan culture and thousands of years of history are at your fingertips.

Relaxed Pace: The pace of life here is slow and relaxed; enjoy long lunches, siesta, and lots of wandering.

Affordability: This trip can be done on a budget without sacrificing quality.

Tracy Carmen Watkin

Bonus Book

50 THINGS TO KNOW ABOUT PACKING LIGHT FOR TRAVEL

Pack the Right Way Every Time

Author: Manidipa
Bhattacharyya

Tracy Carmen Watkin

Edited by Melanie Howthorne

Introduction

*He who would travel happily
must travel light.*

-Antoine de Saint-Exupéry

Travel takes you to different places from seas and mountains to deserts and much more. In your travels you get to interact with different people and their cultures. You will, however, enjoy the sights and interact positively with these new people even more, if you are travelling light.

When you travel light your mind can be free from worry about your belongings. You do not have to spend precious vacation time waiting for your luggage to arrive after a long flight. There is be no chance of your bags going missing and the best part is that you need not pay a fee for checked baggage.

People who have mastered this art of packing light will root for you to take only one carry-on, wherever you go. However, many people can find it really hard to pack light. More so if you are travelling with children. Differentiating between "must have" and "just in case" items is the starting point. There will be ample shopping avenues at your destination which are just waiting to be explored.

Tracy Carmen Watkin

This book will show you 'packing' in a new 'light' –
pun intended – and help you to embrace light
packing practices for all of your future travels.

Off to packing!

Dedication

I dedicate this book to all the travel buffs that I know,
who have given me great insights into the contents of
their backpacks.

About The Author

Manidipa Bhattacharyya is a creative writer and editor, with an education in English literature and Linguistics. After working in the IT industry for seven long years she decided to call it quits and follow her heart instead. Manidipa has been ghost writing, editing, proof reading and doing secondary research services for many story tellers and article writers for about three years. She stays in Kolkata, India with her husband and a busy two year old. In her own time Manidipa enjoys travelling, photography and writing flash fiction.

Manidipa believes in travelling light and never carries anything that she couldn't haul herself on a trip. However, travelling with her child changed the scenario. She seemed to carry the entire world with her for the baby on the first two trips. But good sense prevailed and she is again working her way to becoming a light traveler, this time with a kid.

Tracy Carmen Watkin

The Right Travel Gear

1. Choose Your Travel Gear Carefully

While selecting your travel gear, pick items that are light weight, durable and most importantly, easy to carry. There are cases with wheels so you can drag them along – these are usually on the heavy side because of the trolley. Alternatively a backpack that you can carry comfortably on your back, or even a duffel bag that you can carry easily by hand or sling across your body are also great options. Whatever you choose, one thing to keep in mind is that the luggage itself should not weigh a ton, this will give you the flexibility to bring along one extra pair of shoes if you so desire.

2. Carry The Minimum Number Of Bags

Selecting light weight luggage is not everything. You need to restrict the number of bags you carry as well. One carry-on size bag is ideal for light travel. Most carriers allow one cabin baggage plus one purse, handbag or camera bag as long as it slides under the seat in front. So technically, you can carry two items of luggage without checking them in.

3. Pack One Extra Bag

Always pack one extra empty bag along with your essential items. This could be a very light weight duffel bag or even a sturdy tote bag which takes up minimal space. In the event that you end up buying a lot of souvenirs, you already have a handy bag to stuff all that into and do not have to spend time hunting for an appropriate bag.

I'm very strict with my packing and have everything in its right place. I never change a rule. I hardly use anything in the hotel room. I wheel my own wardrobe in and that's it.

Charlie Watts

Clothes & Accessories

4. Plan Ahead

Figure out in advance what you plan to do on your trip. That will help you to pick that one dress you need for the occasion. If you are going to attend a wedding then you have to carry formal wear. If not, you can ditch the gown for something lighter that will be comfortable during long walks or on the beach.

5. Wear That Jacket

Remember that wearing items will not add extra luggage for your air travel. So wear that bulky jacket that you plan to carry for your trip. This saves space and can also help keep you warm during the chilly flight.

6. Mix and Match

Carry clothes that can be interchangeably used to reinvent your look. Find one top that goes well with a couple of pairs of pants or skirts. Use tops, shirts and jackets wisely along with other accessories like a scarf or a stole to create a new look.

7. Choose Your Fabric Wisely

Stuffing clothes in cramped bags definitely takes its toll which results in wrinkles. It is best to carry wrinkle free, synthetic clothes or merino tops. This will eliminate the need for that small iron you usually bring along.

8. Ditch Clothes Pack Underwear

Pack more underwear and socks. These are the things that will give you a fresh feel even if you do not get a chance to wear fresh clothes. Moreover these are easy to wash and can be dried inside the hotel room itself.

9. Choose Dark Over Light

While picking your clothes choose dark coloured ones. They are easy to colour coordinate and can last longer before needing a wash. Accidental food spills and dirt from the road are less visible on darker clothes.

10. Wear Your Jeans

Take only one pair of Jeans with you, which you should wear on the flight. Remember to pick a pair that can be worn for sightseeing trips and is equally eloquent for dinner. You can add variety by adding light weight cargoes and chinos.

11. Carry Smart Accessories

The right accessory can give you a fresh look even with the same old dress. An intelligent neck-piece, a couple of bright scarves, stoles or a sarong can be used in a number of ways to add variety to your clothing. These light weight beauties can double up as a nursing cover, a light blanket, beach wear, a modesty cover for visiting places of worship, and also makes for an enthralling game of peek-a-boo.

12. Learn To Fold Your Garments

Seasoned travellers all swear by rolling their clothes for compact and wrinkle free packing. Bundle packing, where you roll the clothes around a central object as if tying it up, is also a popular method of compact and wrinkle free packing. Stacking folded clothes one on top of another is a big no-no as it makes creases extreme and they are difficult to get rid of without ironing.

13. Wash Your Dirty Laundry

One of the ways to avoid carrying loads of clothes is to wash the clothes you carry. At some places you might get to use the laundry services or a Laundromat but if you are in a pinch, best solution is to wash them yourself. If that is the plan then carrying quick drying clothes is highly recommended, which most often also happen to be the wrinkle free variety.

14. Leave Those Towels Behind

Regular towels take up a lot of space, are heavy and take ages to dry out. If you are staying at hotels they will provide you with towels anyway. If you are travelling to a remote place, where the availability of towels look doubtful, carry a light weight travel towel of viscose material to do the job.

15. Use A Compression Bag

Compression bags are getting lots of recommendation now days from regular travellers. These are useful for saving space in your luggage when you have to pack bulky dresses. While packing for the return trip, get help from the hotel staff to arrange a vacuum cleaner.

Footwear

16. Put On Your Hiking Boots

If you have plans to go hiking or trekking during your trip, you will need those bulky hiking boots. The best way to carry them is to wear them on flight to save space and luggage weight. You can remove the boots once inside and be comfortable in your socks.

17. Picking The Right Shoes

Shoes are often the bulkiest items, along with being the dainty if you are a female. They need care and take up a lot of space in your luggage. It is advisable therefore to pick shoes very carefully. If you plan to do a lot of walking and site seeing, then wearing a pair of comfortable walking shoes are a must. For more formal occasions you can carry durable, light weight flats which will not take up much space.

18. Stuff Shoes

If you happen to pack a pair of shoes, ensure you utilize their hollow insides. Tuck small items like rolled up socks or belts to save space. They will also be easy to find.

Toiletries
19. Stashing Toiletries

Carry only absolute necessities. Airline rules dictate that for one carry-on bag, liquids and gels must be in 3.4 ounce (100ml) bottles or less, and must be packed in a one quart zip-lock bag. If you are planning to stay in a hotel, the basic things will be provided for you. It's best is to buy the rest from the local market at your destination.

20. Take Along Tampons

Tampons are a hard to find item in a lot of countries. Figure out how many you need and pack accordingly. For longer stays you can buy them online and have them delivered to where you are staying.

21. Get Pampered Before You Travel

Some avid travellers suggest getting a pedicure and manicure just the day before travelling. This not only gives you a well kept look, you also save the trouble of packing nail polish. Remember, every little bit of weight reduced adds up.

Electronics
22. Lugging Along Electronics

Electronics have a large role to play in our lives today. Most of us cannot imagine our lives away from our phones, laptops or tablets. However while travelling, one must consider the amount of weight these electronics add to our luggage. Thankfully smart phones come along with all the essentials tools like a camera, email access, picture editing tools and more. They are smart to the point of eliminating the need to carry multiple gadgets. Choose a smart phone that suits all your requirements and travel with the world in your palms or pocket.

23. Reduce the Number of Chargers

If you do travel with multiple electronic devices, you will have to bear the additional burden of carrying all their chargers too. Check if a single charger can be used for multiple devices. You might also consider investing in a pocket charger. These small devices support multiple devices while keeping you charged on the go.

24. Travel Friendly Apps

Along with smart phones come numerous apps, which are immensely helpful in our travels. You name it and you have an app for it at hand – take pictures, sharing with friends and family, torch to light dark roads, maps, checking flight/train times, find hotels and many other things. Use these smart alternatives to traditional items like books to eliminate weight and save space.

I get ideas about what's essential when packing my suitcase.

-Diane von Furstenberg

Travelling With Kids

25. Bring Along the Stroller

Kids might enjoy walking for a while but they soon
tire out and a stroller is the just the right thing for
them to rest in while you continue your tour. Strollers
also double duty as a luggage carrier and shopping
bag holder. Remember to pick a light weight, easy to
handle brand of stroller. Better yet, find out in
advance if you can rent a stroller at your destination.

26. Bring Only Enough Diapers for Your Trip

Diapers take up a lot of space and add to the weight
of your luggage. Therefore it is advisable to carry just
enough diapers to last through the trip and a few for
afterwards, till you buy fresh stock at your
destination. Unless of course you are travelling to a
really remote area, in which case you have no choice
but to carry the load. Otherwise diapers are something
you will find pretty easily.

27. Take Only A Couple Of Toys

Children are easily attracted by new things in their environment. While travelling they will find numerous 'new' objects to scrutinize and play with. Packing just one favorite toy is enough, or if there is no favorite toy leave out all of them in favor of stories or imaginary games.

28. Carry Kid Friendly Snacks

Create a small snack counter in your bag to store away quick bites for those sudden hunger pangs. Depending on the child's age this could include chocolates, raisins, dry fruits, granola bars or biscuits. Also keep a bottle of water handy for your little one. These things do not add much weight and can be adjusted in a handbag or knapsack.

29. Games to Carry

Create some travel specific, imaginary games if you have slightly grown up children, like spot the attractions. Keep a coloring book and colors handy for in-flight or hotel time. Apps on your smart phone can keep the children engaged with cartoons and story books. Older children are often entertained by games available on phones or tablets. This cuts the weight of luggage down while keeping the kids entertained.

30. Let the Kids Carry Their Load

A good thing is to start early sharing of responsibilities. Let your child pick a bag of his or her choice and pack it themselves. Keep tabs on what they are stuffing in their bags by asking if they will be using that item on the trip. It could start out being just an entertainment bag initially but with growing years they will learn to sort the useful from the superfluous. Children as little as four can maneuver a small trolley suitcase like a pro- their experience in pull along toys credit. If you are worried that you may be pulling it for them, you may want to start with a backpack.

31. Decide on Location for Children to Sleep

While on a trip you might not always get a crib at your destination, and carrying one will make life all the more difficult. Instead call ahead to see if there are any cribs or roll out beds for children. You may even put blankets on the floor. Weave them a story about camping and they will gladly sleep without any trouble.

32. Get Baby Products Delivered At Your Destination

If you are absolutely paranoid about not getting your favourite variety of diaper or brand of baby food, check out online stores like amazon.com for services in your destination city. You can buy things online ahead of your travel and get them delivered to your hotel upon arrival.

33. Feeding Needs Of Your Infants

If you are travelling with a breastfed infant, you save the trouble of carrying bottles and bottle sanitization kits. For special food, or medications, you may need to call ahead to make sure you have a refrigerator where you are staying.

34. Feeding Needs of Your Toddler

With the progression from infancy to toddler, their dietary requirements too evolve. You will have to pack some snacks for travelling time. Fresh fruits and vegetables can be purchased at your destination. Most of the cities you travel to in whichever part of the world, will have baby food products and formulas, available at the local drug-store or the supermarket.

35. Picking Clothes for Your Baby

Contrary to popular belief, babies can do without many changes of clothes. At the most pack 2 outfits per day. Pack mix and match type clothes for your little one as well. Pick things which are comfortable to wear and quick to dry.

36. Selecting Shoes for Your Baby

Like outfits, kids can make do with two pairs of comfortable shoes. If you can get some water resistant shoes it will be best. To expedite drying wet shoes, you can stuff newspaper in them then wrap them with newspaper and leave them to dry overnight.

37. Keep One Change of Clothes Handy

Travelling with kids can be tricky. Keep a change of clothes for the kids and mum handy in your purse or tote bag. This takes a bit of space in your hand luggage but comes extremely handy in case there are any accidents or spills.

38. Leave Behind Baby Accessories

Baby accessories like their bed, bath tub, car seat, crib etc. should be left at home. Many hotels provide a crib on request, while car seats can be borrowed from friends or rented. Babies can be given a bath in the hotel sink or even in the adult bath tub with a little bit of water. If you bring a few bath toys, they can be used in the bath, pool, and out of water. They can also be sanitized easily in the sink.

39. Carry a Small Load Of Plastic Bags

With children around there are chances of a number of soiled clothes and diapers. These plastic bags help to sort the dirt from the clean inside your big bag. These are very light weight and come in handy to other carry stuff as well at times.

Pack with a Purpose

40. Packing for Business Trips

One neutral-colored suit should suffice. It can be paired with different shirts, ties and accessories for different occasions. One pair of black suit pants could be worn with a matching jacket for the office or with a snazzy top for dinner.

41. Packing for A Cruise

Most cruises have formal dinners, and that formal dress usually takes up a lot of space. However you might find a tuxedo to rent. For women, a short black dress with multiple accessory options will do the trick.

42. Packing for A Long Trip Over Different Climates

The secret packing mantra for travel over multiple climates is layering. Layering traps air around your body creating insulation against the cold. The same light t-shirt that is comfortable in a warmer climate can be the innermost layer in a colder climate.

Reduce Some More Weight

43. Leave Precious Things At Home

Things that you would hate to lose or get damaged leave them at home. Precious jewelry, expensive gadgets or dresses, could be anything. You will not require these on your trip. Leave them at home and spare the load on your mind.

44. Send Souvenirs by Mail

If you have spent all your money on purchasing souvenirs, carrying them back in the same bag that you brought along would be difficult. Either pack everything in another bag and check it in the airport or get everything shipped to your home. Use an international carrier for a secure transit, but this could be more expensive than the checking fees at the airport.

45. Avoid Carrying Books

Books equal to weight. There are many reading apps which you can download on your smart phone or tab. Plus there are gadgets like Kindle and Nook that are thinner and lighter alternatives to your regular book.

Check, Get, Set, Check Again

46. Strategize Before Packing

Create a travel list and prepare all that you think you need to carry along. Keep everything on your bed or floor before packing and then think through once again – do I really need that? Any item that meets this question can be avoided. Remove whatever you don't really need and pack the rest.

47. Test Your Luggage

Once you have fully packed for the trip take a test trip with your luggage. Take your bags and go to town for window shopping for an hour. If you enjoy your hour long trip it is good to go, if not, go home and reduce the load some more. Repeat this test till you hit the right weight.

48. Add a Roll Of Duct Tape

You might wonder why, when this book has been talking about reducing stuff, we're suddenly asking you to pack something totally unusual. This is because when you have limited supplies, duct tape is immensely helpful for small repairs – a broken bag, leaking zip-lock bag, broken sunglasses, you name it and duct tape can fix it, temporarily.

49. List of Essential Items

Even though the emphasis is on packing light, there are things which have to be carried for any trip. Here is our list of essentials:

• Passport/Visa or any other ID

- Any other paper work that might be required on a trip like permits, hotel reservation confirmations etc.

- Medicines – all your prescription medicines and emergency kit, especially if you are travelling with children

- Medical or vaccination records

- Money in foreign currency if travelling to a different country

- Tickets- Email or Message them to your phone

50. Make the Most of Your Trip

Wherever you are going, whatever you hope to do we encourage you to embrace it whole-heartedly. Take in the scenery, the culture and above all, enjoy your time away from home.

*On a long journey even a straw
weighs heavy.*

-Spanish Proverb

>TOURIST

Tracy Carmen Watkin

Packing and Planning Tips

A Week before Leaving

- Arrange for someone to take care of pets and water plants

- •Stop mail and newspaper

- Notify Credit Card companies where you are going.

- Change your thermostat settings

- Car inspected, oil is changed, and tires have the correct pressure.

- Passports and id is up to date.

- Pay bills.

- Copy important items and download travel Apps.

- Start collecting small bills for tips

Right Before Leaving

- Clean out refrigerator.

- Empty garbage cans.

- Lock windows.

- Make sure you have the right ID with you.

- Bring cash for tips.

- Remember travel documents.

- Lock door behind you.

- Remember wallet.

- Unplug items in house and pack chargers.

Tracy Carmen Watkin

Read other Greater Than a Tourist Books

Greater Than a Tourist San Miguel de Allende Guanajuato Mexico: 50 Travel Tips from a Local by Tom Peterson

Greater Than a Tourist – Lake George Area New York USA: 50 Travel Tips from a Local by Janine Hirschklau

Greater Than a Tourist – Monterey California United States: 50 Travel Tips from a Local by Katie Begley

Greater Than a Tourist – Chanai Crete Greece: 50 Travel Tips from a Local by Dimitra Papagrigoraki

Greater Than a Tourist – The Garden Route Western Cape Province South Africa: 50 Travel Tips from a Local by Li-Anne McGregor van Aardt

Greater Than a Tourist – Sevilla Andalusia Spain: 50 Travel Tips from a Local by Gabi Gazon

Greater Than a Tourist – Kota Bharu Kelantan Malaysia: 50 Travel Tips from a Local by Aditi Shukla

Children's Book: Charlie the Cavalier Travels the World by Lisa Rusczyk

Tracy Carmen Watkin

> TOURIST

Visit Greater Than a Tourist for Free Travel Tips
http://GreaterThanATourist.com

Sign up for the Greater Than a Tourist Newsletter for
discount days, new books, and travel information:
http://eepurl.com/cxspyf

Follow us on Facebook for tips, images, and ideas:
https://www.facebook.com/GreaterThanATourist

Follow us on Pinterest for travel tips and ideas:
http://pinterest.com/GreaterThanATourist

Follow us on Instagram for beautiful travel images:
http://Instagram.com/GreaterThanATourist

Tracy Carmen Watkin

> TOURIST

Please leave your honest review of this book on Amazon and Goodreads. Please send your feedback to GreaterThanaTourist@gmail.com as we continue to improve the series. Thank you. We appreciate your positive and constructive feedback. Thank you.

Tracy Carmen Watkin

NOTES

Tracy Carmen Watkin